A WORD and
A $HAKE

Communication Series for the Texting Generation

A WORD and A $HAKE

Interview Storytelling Skills for GenText™

Elaine Rosenblum, JD

BOOKLOGIX
Alpharetta, GA

Although the author and publisher have made every effort to ensure that the information in this book was correct at the time of first publication, the author and publisher do not assume and hereby disclaim any liability to any party for any loss, damage, or disruption caused by errors or omissions, whether such errors or omissions result from negligence, accident, or any other cause. The author has tried to recreate events, locations, and conversations from her memories of them. In some instances, in order to maintain their anonymity, the author has changed the names of individuals and places. She may also have changed some identifying characteristics and details such as physical attributes, occupations, and places of residence.

Copyright © 2018 by Elaine Rosenblum

All rights reserved. No part of this book may be reproduced or transmitted in any form or by any means, electronic or mechanical, including photocopying, recording, or any information storage and retrieval system, without permission in writing from the publisher. For more information, address BookLogix, c/o Permissions Department, 1264 Old Alpharetta Rd., Alpharetta, GA 30005.

ISBN: 978-1-63183-332-8 - Paperback
eISBN: 978-1-63183-333-5 - ePub
eISBN: 978-1-63183-334-2 - mobi

Printed in the United States of America   011119

⊛This paper meets the requirements of ANSI/NISO Z39.48-1992 (Permanence of Paper)

GenText®, GenTexters®, and ProForm U® are registered trademarks of Elaine Rosenblum
Cover art by Jordana Slawin

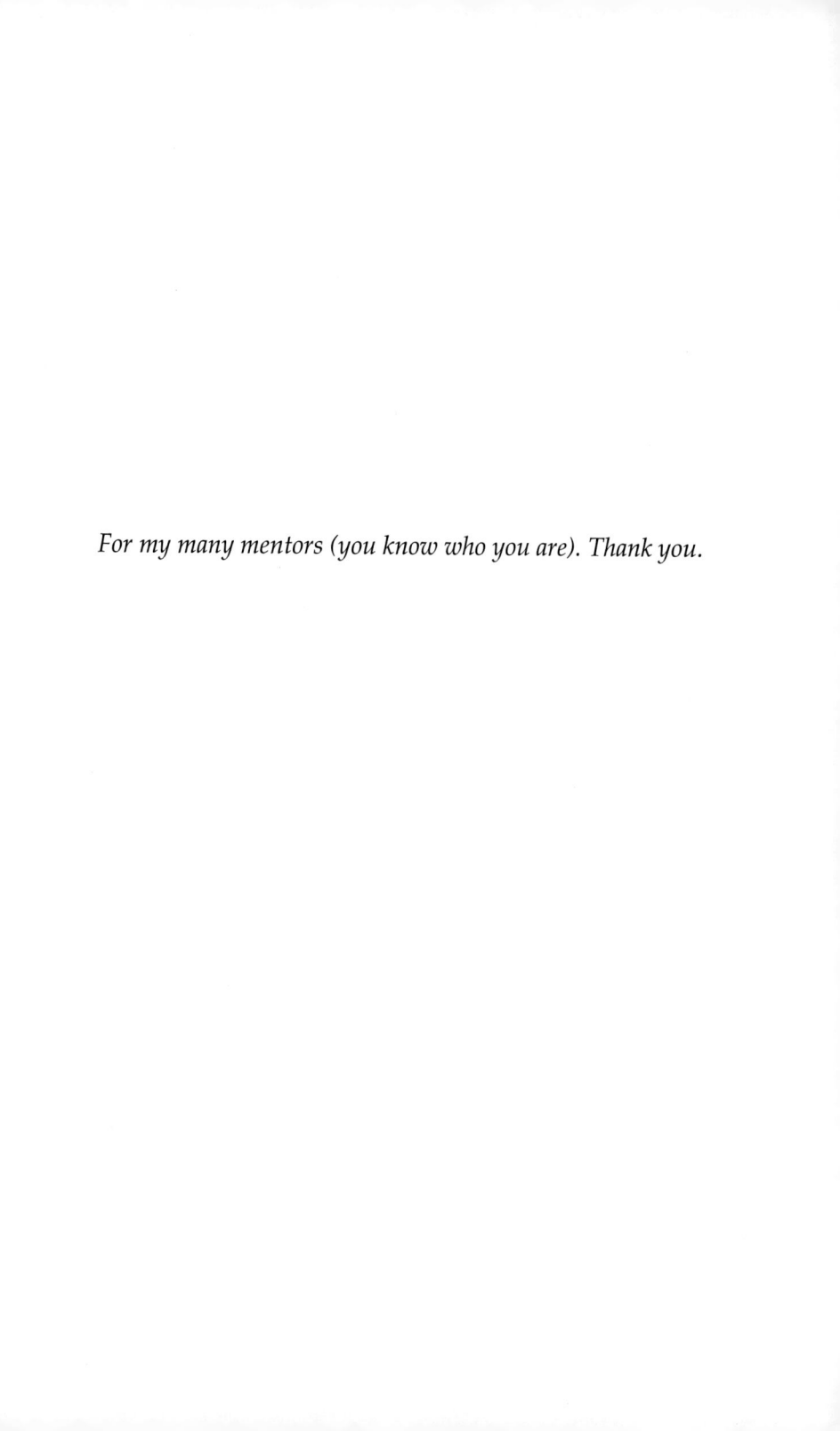

For my many mentors (you know who you are). Thank you.

You are only as good as your word.
—English Proverb

Contents

Foreword	xi
Preface	xiii
Acknowledgments	xv
Introduction: Everyone's Scared	xvii

Chapter 1   1
   College, Scholarship, Internship, or Graduate School Interviews—It Won't Get You In, but It Could Keep You Out

Chapter 2   13
   The Internship—Getting Your Feet Wet

Chapter 3   21
   The Job Interview—Taking the Brag Out by Telling Your Story

Chapter 4   41
   The Résumé—Articulating U on Paper

Chapter 5   49
   Speaking the Language of Negotiation

Chapter 6   55
   Are You My Mentor?—Knowing People Who Know

Chapter 7   65
   Speaking Up and Out

Chapter 8   71
   Cuz, Like, Do I Have to Use SAT Words?

Appendix   75
    Sample Cover Letter   77
    Elaine Rosenblum Résumé   79
    Sample Achievement Résumé   82
    Sample Interview Thank-You Note   83
    Appropriate Interview Attire for Men and Women   84

Foreword

The first time I met Elaine Rosenblum, I instantly knew I found a kindred spirit. While it usually takes time for trust and friendship to build and blossom, my gut instinct told me, "This is a woman I will know my whole life." A multilayered bond had taken hold professionally and personally.

Elaine has this uncanny ability—you could call it a gift—to converse and be a true storyteller. As a journalist and professional storyteller, I'd met my match. Elaine can paint an incredible picture with words, using the intonation and colorful detail of, well, a pro.

As a journalist, I've been telling stories for more than twenty-five years. I'm also mom to two GenTexters. If you are on your way to college, a budding or young professional, or you've spawned a GenTexter or two, the book you're holding is a treasure in hand.

In this gem, you'll learn in snap speed how to conduct and present yourself in the game of interviewing and job landing in our über-competitive academic race and workplace. The magic and sweet spot of differentiating yourself is dead center in the heart of storytelling, and Elaine uses her deep knowledge of the educational and professional spaces to teach you just how to tell your story so that interviewers will sit up, take notice, and admit or hire you. Read her stories and advice, hold onto this book, refer to it often, and you'll be well-prepared for lift-off and ascent to Planet Professional.

Believe me, I know a thing or two about producing stories and preparing professionals. From years in network control rooms, including on September 11 as CNN's executive news producer, to coaching CEOs to go on TV and tell their stories, Elaine "gets it." Her book is your "go to" for writing a résumé that speaks volumes and interviewing to land a college or grad-school seat, scholarship, internship, and ultimately get a job, one carefully worded story at a time.

—Jodi Fleisig
Emmy Award–Winning TV News Sr. Executive Producer
Strategic Media Consultant
Atlanta, GA

Preface

I wrote this book because I was very lucky. I did not have to seek out my professional mentors, Barry Silverman and David Cooper; they found me. Both recognized my potential and took me under their wings. Barry held my hand through interviews, guided me as to what to say in voicemails, and advised me on salary and general negotiation strategy. David simply asked me what I actually said when an interviewer asked the most frequently asked interview question: "Walk me through your résumé." My rough, hesitant, half-baked answer made him generously sit down with me and draft a proper interview script.

Had each not done so, I would have never gotten three Big Apple job offers in three weeks and received the invaluable professional grooming that came from working my way up in the toughest boot camp there is, the New York City corporate world. The rewards of that training gave me the courage to go to law school, learn to mediate, and embark on three successful entrepreneurial ventures: Courageous Conversation, Access Test Prep & Tutoring, and ProForm U.

I wrote this book to compile and share the professional wisdom imparted to me from Barry, David, and so many others who took the time to answer my questions, dry my tears, and pull me aside to give me feedback that I needed to hear. From my years working in the highly competitive

Elaine Rosenblum, JD

college-prep and standardized-test-prep industries, I learned that GenText, in particular, needs guidance in mastering interviewing as a baseline skill. I share these stories so you can avoid common mistakes, follow my lead, and know what I have come to learn—that standing on your own two feet through your own hard work, sweat, and tears is much better than power; it is empowering. But first, you have to land a classroom seat and a job.

It starts with a word and a shake.

Acknowledgments

So many people have influenced my career success. The first is the smartest man I know, my husband, Charles. Thank you for your continued wisdom, partnership, support, and for being my human dictionary, encyclopedia, and calculator.

To my favorite mentee and son, Nelson, who inspires me to be a better mentor and teacher each and every day.

To my students and clients, thank you for the privilege of sharing in your journeys, occasional failures, and many successes. It is music to my ears when you call (or more likely text) to say "I got in," "I got the scholarship," "I got the internship," "I got the job," and "I got more money!" It is simply the most rewarding work I have ever done.

To Dinora, Nelson's other mother. Without you, I could do none of this.

To the queen of mentors, Carol. We luckily found each other. There are no words.

Thank you to the team at BookLogix for your mentorship and nurturing in every scary step of birthing this book.

To Lisa Matheson and Melanie Levs for editing my writing. I am better because of your ability to strike through extra verbiage.

Thanks to Brent Yamatto for advising me to go for it—all of it.

To Jordana Slawin. Thank you for the beautiful cover art. Your keen artistic eye nailed it.

Lastly, thank you to my mom, Sandra Lee, for having the guts to start college at age thirty-nine. Your example spoke to me loud and clear: "Elaine, of course you can go to law school at age thirty-two!"

Without the confidence from my professional success and the grounding in logic that I gained from my legal education, this book would never have been written.

Introduction: Everyone's Scared

I heard that Jay Z has a piece of art hanging in his office waiting room that sums up a good way to think about interviewing. It reads: *Everyone's scared.* I say, if everyone is scared, then there's nothing to be afraid of, right?

Take it from me. I have worked with many highly successful people and enjoyed a great deal of success myself. Everyone—and I mean *everyone*—is, at times, scared. I vividly remember being petrified at the thought of going to and graduating from college. I knew little or nothing about how to interview and get in, get an internship, or get a real job.

You are not alone. We all have fears and anxieties (including the person interviewing you). Accept that being scared is normal and makes you human. Take a deep breath and consider these ways to think strategically about the art of interviewing. It starts and ends with a word and shake.

Chapter 1
College, Scholarship, Internship, or Graduate School Interviews—It Won't Get You In, but It Could Keep You Out

In the past ten years, neuroscientists have learned more about how the brain processes information than we've known in all of civilization. And the consensus is that the brain is wired for story. We think in narrative, we develop narratives about ourselves and the world around us, and we enjoy consuming information in the form of story.[1]

If you think about it, the purpose of SATs, college, internships, and job interviews is to land a job and ultimately earn a living. It's time to invest in a skill that you will repeat over and over into the future. It's never too early to learn and master this lifelong skill, a.k.a. interviewing!

Depending on what colleges you are applying to, you may be asked to do an interview. Ivy League and some other competitive schools like Georgetown University and

---

[1] Carmine Gallo, "What Richard Branson and Phil Knight Teach Us About Brand Storytelling," Inc., June 27, 2017, https://www.inc.com/carmine-gallo/your-company-needs-a-chief-storyteller-like-richard-branson-and-phil-knight.html.

Washington University in St. Louis typically require an alumni interview, as do some scholarships and graduate schools. If you're visiting a campus, I also recommend setting up a meeting with the admissions office, which, in a sense, is an interview.

Why do these schools conduct interviews? The purpose of meeting in person is to understand:

- If you and the college or school are "a good fit"
- What your personality is like, and if it complements the culture of the interviewing school's community and educational goals for its graduates
- What kind of student you are, and how you handle yourself under pressure
- If other students would like living and participating in class discussions with you

In essence, the interviewer is seeking the answer to the question "Who are you, prospective student?" Often, these interviews are conducted with an alumni of the college or university who lives in your area, who will then fill out a report and send it back to the admissions department with his or her thoughts about you as an applicant. Scholarship interviews, on the other hand, are typically with a panel of professors, admissions officers, and alumni involved with the scholarship. Graduate school interviews are typically conducted on campus by admissions officers.

If you meet with the admissions department during a college visit, the representative will put a comment in your application folder noting your interest in the school—and hopefully your "good fit" status, assuming you read on and take my interview advice!

The alumnus interviewer will likely email you to set up an appointment to meet somewhere, often a "neutral" location (not associated with the university) like a coffee shop or his or her office. You will:

- Prepare ahead of time, not the night before. And by "prepare," I mean research the university's website, taking note of key language describing the type of student and culture there, and perhaps even research the person who is interviewing you (if you are given the name beforehand) so you can tailor your comments and questions to the interviewer. Looking your interviewer up on Google or LinkedIn, then asking a question demonstrating that you did this research, is a smart interview strategy.
- Dress appropriately (see Appendix page 84).
- Arrive early so you have time to spit out your gum, turn off your phone, and pop a breath mint.
- Introduce yourself to your interviewer with a firm handshake (but don't cut off circulation).
- Make eye contact.
- Answer questions fully.

Sounds simple, right? It can be . . . if you keep reading!

This interview is important. It won't get you *in* the college of your choice, but it certainly can keep you *out*. It does hold some weight, and it makes sense that you, like most people, would be nervous about being interviewed because, of course, we all are uncomfortable with the idea of being judged. Also, since you have grown up texting on your smartphone and interacting so frequently online, having a face-to-face conversation with an older adult may be a little scary. Advice that I consistently repeat may sound like common sense, but it's worth repeating. So, here goes:

1. Spit out your gum before your interviewer even lays eyes on you.
2. Turn off your phone and put it out of sight. If you are expecting an emergency phone call—for example, your mother is having surgery and you want an update—it is appropriate to say to your interviewer, "I know I'm not supposed to have my phone out during my interview, but my mother is in the middle of surgery right now and my father plans to call me as soon as she's in recovery. I know that I'll feel better when I know that she is in recovery. Thank you for understanding." If you are dealing with a situation like this, the interviewer will not only empathize (interviewers have parents and children, too!) but he or she will likely be impressed that you prepared and anticipated their view of your phone's appearance. In addition, if you are a little "shaky" in the interview, the interviewer may just cut you some slack since you had a parent in surgery at interview time. That said, do *not* make up such a story. The interviewer will see right through this ploy.

THE IMPORTANCE OF TINY MINTS

I also often tell students to buy some of those tiny mints to freshen your breath before an interview (and therefore eliminate gum altogether). Why tiny ones? Let's say you arrive early (as you are supposed to do) and you are sucking on a mint, when the interviewer spots you and walks over to introduce him or herself. With a tiny mint in your mouth, all you have to do is swallow it, and you are instantly more professional.

Your breath is fresh, your mouth is clear, your handshake is firm, your eyes are on your interviewer. So, what will he or she likely ask? And, more importantly, how do you answer?

Here are some questions that you are almost sure to encounter:

> Walk me through your résumé/tell me about yourself.

The interview is like telling a story. You are sharing your story with a person who can help your application get noticed. By giving the interviewer a peek into your life story, you provide insight into who you are and how you can contribute to their alma mater or college (in the case of an admissions or scholarship interview).

Therefore, this common question (often the first one) is a given and a bit of a test—prepare for it! Make sure you don't start rambling and regurgitate your résumé. Again, it's about being prepared and telling your story with a beginning, middle, and end. Your "tell me about yourself" or "walk me through your résumé" answer should be an overview, the highlights of your experiences, and a sentence or three (or "elevator speech") about who you are.

For example, here is my elevator speech, or the way I'd describe myself in the time it takes to ride an elevator with someone: "My background is in marketing, law, education, and entrepreneurship. I've started three companies. I found a way to take those four professional skill sets and combine them to mentor students and professionals to articulate, negotiate, collaborate, and therefore innovate. I also deliver keynote speeches on related topics."

Here is one of my student's elevator speeches: "I am an academic honors varsity-football captain. I spent last summer working in a solar-panel business and loved learning about how solar technology is being used to power trucks and car batteries. The summer before that, I worked in an entrepreneurial incubator. Something I'm most proud of is that I changed the culture on my high school varsity-football team. I am interested in ABC University because it offers me the opportunity to further my business-and-entrepreneurial interests while serving as an on-campus change leader."

Notice that the student planted a "seed" at the close of his comments. The seed is a kernel of information that your interviewer will surely pick up on. His seed is his comment about changing the culture on his high school varsity-football team. "Seed-planting" gives the interviewer a subtle cue as to the next obvious question, and gives you the ability to steer the interviewer to ask questions that you already are prepared to answer! For example, the interviewer likely would ask my student, "How did you change the culture of your high school football team?"

Why do you want to attend this school?

"I have good grades" is a common answer. You would not be in the interview unless your grades were good. You know in your heart this is a college that is special, but that is not really an answer, either; it's too general. What does "special" really mean?

The interviewer wants to know how you fit in the student profile (or character and potential) that the school is looking to shape. The goal here is to align your skills and achievements with the school's value system. It is worth it to craft your answer to this predictable FAQ on paper and commit it to memory. Your answer does not need to be word-for-word as you wrote it, though; you want to sound like a human, not a memorizing robot.

One strategic way to answer this question is to read very carefully the "Mission" or "About" tabs on the school's website, and pick out buzz words and phrases. What adjectives are used to describe the school, student community, and graduates? Think about the experiences and skills you yourself have that match those attributes, and plan your answer accordingly. For example, Duke University's website states (underlines are mine): "We believe that _diversity_ fosters _innovation_, _creativity_, and _excellence_, and that it prepares our students to become _leaders_."

Your buzz words are right there. You should talk about how you are:

1. Graduating from the international school (diversity)

2. Fluent in Russian (diversity)
3. Partnering with a smoothie company to serve milkshakes to chemotherapy patients to ward off nausea (innovation)
4. Building an electric minicar from scratch (innovation and creativity)
5. Giving a speech to your entire high school about fear (it takes courage and leadership to put your emotional cards on the table in front of your peers)

What books have you read that you have enjoyed—or not enjoyed—and why?

My generation assumes that you don't read. I say, prove them wrong!

For this question, you definitely can use books you have read for school, but it is even better if you can mention a book that has nothing to do with school but says something about your personality or interests. For example, maybe you read a biography of Steve Jobs. You can then comment about the book, saying something like, "Despite the fact that he was a tough manager, I would have loved to work for him because he was such a creative genius and innovative thinker."

I often recommend to my students a book by Hollywood producer Brian Grazer called *A Curious Mind*, which is about the importance of being continually curious. Grazer initiated conversations with people who fascinate him, such as John Nash, the real-life Princeton professor who inspired Grazer's movie *A Beautiful Mind*. In the

8

book, Grazer shares that he learned so much by asking interesting people questions about their lives and how they think. If you read it and share this with the interviewer, it shows that you might do the same when you meet people on campus.

College and grad school are all about learning through discussion and conversation. Take time to read books that speak to creativity, innovation, leadership, and curiosity.

What's your greatest weakness?

With this question, interviewers want to hear humility and self-awareness, so think about your "weakness" as something you already are looking to change. Start your answer with "Something I'm working on is . . . " For example, one of my students, during his college interview, answered that he is a very slow reader. This sounds like it could be a negative for a prospective college student, but in fact, his answer is creative and demonstrates problem-solving skills. He explained that to compensate for the fact that he reads slowly, he downloads books on audio and listens to them because he identifies as an auditory learner. For textbooks that are not available via audio, he cuts and pastes portions into an audio-reader app. In his answer, this student showed he was an innovative and creative problem solver, key traits colleges look for today (and this student got into his choice of college).

Tell me about a time you failed.

One young woman told her college interviewer about

a time she got into an accident during her driving test! Being a good driver has nothing to do with being a good college student, and that is why it is a good story. Also, it's funny, and offers an opportunity to show that you can laugh at yourself and have a strong sense of humor, which could make it easy and fun to live with you as a roommate.

Often, when I share this story with students, they are able to come up with their own funny failure stories they can share in their college interviews. Let your less-serious and vulnerable side show! This reminds the interviewer that you have humility and will be a fun-loving member of the student community.

Tell me about a time that you were a leader.

Leadership is a skill that all interviewers—be it for college, a scholarship, grad school, an internship, or a job—are seeking. A good leadership story can be found on the playing field as a captain or softball pitcher, student council member, camp counselor, in a service organization, or in an extracurricular activity. You do not necessarily have to be in a leadership role; the source and role matter less than the story demonstrating the skill.

A staff writer of a high school student newspaper told a story about noticing the inconsistent grammar among the newspaper articles. She proposed and wrote a grammar guide for the entire newspaper's editorial staff. Although she was not in a leadership position on the editorial team, she demonstrated serious leadership skills by initiating a major improvement in the newspaper end product. Any interviewer at any level of school or the professional arena would welcome this leadership story because it exemplifies attention to detail and problem solving.

In addition to writing out answers to common college interview questions before the interview, there are other ways to prepare. Demonstrate that you know what's going on in the world, including current events and major headlines in the United States and abroad. "It's a shame that there was an earthquake in India" could be one of your comments. "Did you see those pictures online?"

Read reputable sources online or in print. For example, if you are looking to major in business, you should read the front page of the *Wall Street Journal* (in general now and also intentionally on the day of your interview).

Aside from doing your homework on the news, look up the name of the person doing your interview on LinkedIn. Read about what he or she does, and be prepared to ask him or her your own follow-up questions, such as:

1. What was your favorite part of going to this college?
2. How did your experience at ABC University influence your career?
3. (For the admissions officer) What do you think it takes to be a successful student at this school?

Showing interest in the interviewer's career and life after college, as well as his or her connection to the college, enables bonding. If the interviewer is not on LinkedIn, Google him or her. "I read that you raise money for the

ASPCA. I love dogs. How did you get involved with the ASPCA?" This tells your interviewer that you prepared, did your research, and have something in common. People like to talk about themselves, common interests, and most importantly, interviewers LOVE prepared interviewees.

WHAT SHOULD YOU NOT DO?

As important as it is for you to be knowledgeable about current events and news, you do not need to (nor should you) engage in political or other "edgy" topics with your interviewer (unless perhaps you plan to major in political science or a related topic . . . but still, tread lightly). Being politically neutral during the interview is a plus, because you truly do not know who you are talking to. The world is currently too divided to "go there." Alumni interviewers are told to stay away from these issues for the same reasons. Save that talk for when you're a student on campus!

The bottom line during a college interview? These interviewers are not trying to trick you, but the process is competitive. They are looking for interesting reasons why they *can* recommend or admit you. So, be interested in the school and interesting as a person (to your interviewer).

When the interview is over and you've extended yet another firm handshake, walked away, and gotten back in the car or outside, *only then* can you pop in that gum or gigantic mint. Also, smile because you just nailed interviewing, a skill you will need for years to come. And, don't forget to write a thank-you note within twenty-four hours (see more on thank-you notes on Appendix page 83).

Chapter 2
The Internship—Getting Your Feet Wet

Congratulations! You're in college, you're exploring, and you're figuring out who you want to be in the future and what you want to do as a career. Maybe your first summer after freshman year you were a camp counselor, or went back to your high school retail job, or decided to wait tables so you could live at the beach. Now, though, you are getting a bit deeper into your college career and perhaps major. It's time to think about that *other* career—the one you need to embark on when you graduate so you can, you know, earn money.

This glance toward the future often comes in the form of an internship. By "internship," I mean you work in a company or organization, sometimes for free, so you can learn what life is like in a particular industry or role in the professional world.

Why is getting coffee or making copies actually a good thing?

Some people associate internships with grunt work, like getting coffee, making copies, or running errands for higher-ups. That is a stereotype—though, because you are an intern and likely unpaid, you may be required to take on tasks that you see as irrelevant to the work of the company. Coffee and copies are likely on the menu; however, they also are an opportunity to speak to those whose shoes you might want to walk in. These so-called "menial" tasks are excuses to strike up a conversation and bond with a person who can offer you a job, or at least put in a good word for you. Coffee is an opportunity to ask, "What do you like best about this e-commerce merchandising job?" or "What made you choose a career in fashion?" Coffee is the chance to say, "It would be my dream to work in sports marketing after college."

Though you are not rewarded for your efforts with money, the professional experience, exposure, networking connections, and insight you gain are invaluable.

One of my students was attending Parsons in New York City. She got lucky and interned at Diane von Furstenberg (DVF) for the summer. I advised her to do her grunt work better than other interns, arrive early and stay late, ask for more work, volunteer to do extra projects, and engage in conversations and perhaps a meal with her boss and her boss's boss. My student made herself invaluable to her boss. DVF kept her on beyond her summer internship—for a year and a half—and they paid her the entire time. Upon graduating from Parsons, she was offered a full-time job at DVF corporate.

Why else should you pursue an internship? A lot of young people assume that they have to make an absolute decision about their profession when searching for an internship. But the whole idea of internships is that you are experimenting, researching, and gaining exposure to a variety of industries. If you choose an internship and have a negative experience—because, for example, you spent all day at a desk versus out and about talking to clients—that is good information for your post-graduation job search. You learned that you don't want a desk job. It's just as important to know what you do *not* want to do as it is to know what you *do* want to do.

Internships help you narrow your focus. A common issue for my students and professional clients is that they are overwhelmed by career choices. Internships help you more clearly identify the specific paths that you want to take.

On the other hand, if you have a particular long-term goal—medical school, for example—it is in your best interest to do a medical- or health-related internship over the summer, such as researching in a lab (at this point, research internships are almost a must for medical and dental school applicants). One student I worked with was interested in global women's health, and spent a summer in Africa gathering data for research on women's health in various villages. Another student lived in a leprosy camp in Ghana, testing blood-strip technology for remote geographies. You certainly do not need to go to a developing country, but you can see the advantages to doing something related to your longer-term interest.

One of my dental school applicant clients worked with a volunteer organization that provided free dental care for more than two thousand patients per weekend for those unable to afford dentistry (a big healthcare issue facing the US). After several volunteer stints, he was basically functioning as a dental assistant. This experience not only showed commitment to service, but also served as relevant storytelling for his dental school interviews. My student also told me that the patients were so appreciative to finally be pain-free after months of agonizing dental pain that the work was incredibly rewarding. This "love of clinical dentistry" is music to a dental-school interviewer's ears. PS: my student was admitted to dental school.

You can imagine that when college interns face job interviews after graduation, they could draw on their unique internship experiences as proof of their tenacity, work ethic, and interest in their respective fields.

Speaking of job interviews down the road, like the young woman at DVF I mentioned earlier, internships are a major stepping stone to careers. One student I worked with loved basketball and was interested in sports management. He participated in a two-week sports-marketing introductory program in Las Vegas, where over the course of a couple of weeks during winter break, he learned from, met with, and networked with key sports-industry executives. He made so many connections that he secured a position as a paid manager on his university's basketball team beginning in the fall of his sophomore year. He has continued in the role and will until he graduates.

Another basketball-loving Davidson student was an excellent varsity high school player. He got an on-campus, paid job scrimmaging with his basketball buddies against the Davidson women's varsity basketball team. The friends found a way to be paid and make career connections playing basketball, something they would be doing anyway. Talk about pay to play! The Davidson student's dad told me that he wants to coach women's college basketball as a career. Working out with the Davidson women's team and knowing the Davidson coaches has opened doors for his future career goals.

Both the team manager and scrimmage jobs are related and relevant exposure and work experience, prove reliability (because you have to be on time and accountable in these roles), and provide endless future interview stories for these students.

So, how does one go about obtaining such internship gold? Consider your interests. For example, if you love numbers and are interested in finance, but no one in your family has any connections to that industry, ask a finance professor at your school to introduce you to someone in the industry. Perhaps there is an adjunct professor in the finance department who has a banking day job and whose company could use an intern. Ask your friends and family members to ask around for you, and mention your interest to pretty much everyone with whom you come in contact. You never know when it will pay off!

For example, one young woman already home in Atlanta from college for the summer went with her mother to get a facial. While lying on the aesthetician's table, she mentioned she wanted to get a real estate internship for the summer. The aesthetician actually had a client who was a real estate development executive in need of interns, and a match was made! So, always be talking about your interests, what you want to do, and remember to ask people outright, "Do you know any who does . . . ?"

Another way to secure an internship is to contact the "back office" of a retail establishment or restaurant that you enjoy. Working at a restaurant is not just about serving; there is a corporate component to just about every type of business. If you are a frequent H&M shopper, for example, visit the website and click around in the About or Corporate Headquarters sections, and inquire about internship opportunities (many of these companies may even advertise internship programs under the "Careers" tab on their websites). If you like ice cream, how about checking out the corporate section for the website of Baskin-Robbins, or even an independent shop in your hometown? I know another student who was very creative. Her study flash cards were beautiful. I encouraged her to get a job at a stationery store designing invitations that were printed on-site. She followed my advice and, needless to say, her paid stationery store job looked very good on her Savannah College of Art and Design (SCAD) college application.

An internship provides you with professional experience that you also can speak about in a future job (or internship) interview. While hopefully you are paid, and even if you are not, the transferable skills you gain—industry knowledge, what it's like to work in a professional environment, demonstrating punctuality and work ethic, getting along with coworkers and bosses, managing and being managed, etc.—are priceless.

One summer, a student I worked with did an internship at a solar-energy company owned by the father of a friend. This young man learned about different types of solar panels, how they work, and the various innovations behind these futuristic materials. He was not particularly interested in science, and did not see this internship as a step to a career in the field, but he knew that solar energy was the future, and that knowing about it would give him an *edge* in the future.

He was able to discuss how electric cars would use the inexpensive panels to charge their batteries. Why would he talk about this in an interview? Because to succeed, whether it be gaining an internship, making a positive impression, and/or landing a goal-affirming job, you not only have to be *interested*, but also *interesting*. This young man had entrepreneurial aspirations and a gift for numbers and leadership. Being able to talk about alternative energy and elements of solar science added a whole other fascinating dimension to his interview story.

Landing that internship is step one! Then, once you secure it, you have to actually *work*. This means playing by the rules of the professional game:

1. Dress professionally (see Appendix page 84)
2. Arrive early or on time, and stay until the end of the day
3. Take only your allotted breaks
4. Do not play on your phone AT ALL (in fact, leave it in your car until your break)
5. If you don't know something, ask, and ask respectfully

Do you need to take a day off from work for a doctor's appointment or family commitment? Ask, and then offer to work overtime or come in earlier. This shows your supervisors that even though you are not getting paid, you have a responsible work ethic. Is there a particular project you want to work on? Speak up! You're taking initiative. These "soft skill" details of the job world (punctuality, speaking up, being conscientious about committing to your work hours and hungry for knowledge) are non-negotiable and will serve you well throughout your entire career.

My niece learned this lesson a few summers ago when she interned at a film festival. She was then a student at a prestigious Midwestern school, and came to live with me for the internship. One afternoon, she received a text from a supervisor: "Are you coming?" It was about a meeting she was expected to attend, but there had been some miscommunication. It was nearing rush hour (which in my city lasts almost all afternoon and into the evening), and she needed to drive some twenty-five miles north of the city to make the meeting.

"I'm not going," she told me.

I disagreed. I told her to get in the car and drive up there! I explained that she wanted these people to see her go above and beyond the call of duty and *show up*. After all, if she proved herself, these important corporate leaders would provide stellar recommendation letters for a future film-related or any job that she wanted.

One last thing about internships: If you have an opportunity to impress the higher-ups with your initiative, go for it; you have nothing to lose. Identify those opportunities to distinguish yourself and go the extra mile, and demonstrate to those decision makers that you are willing to "bust your butt" more than anyone else. A common complaint about your generation is that you have little appreciation for work ethic and the hard work that goes into success. I say *be the exception and prove them wrong*! If you are articulate, conscientious, *show up when it's inconvenient*, and take that initiative, you will go far in life. You are in that internship position for a reason; make the most of it.

Chapter 3
The Job Interview—Taking the Brag Out by Telling Your Story

The ability to tell a story with passion, humor, and heart will help build trust.

—Richard Branson

I could not agree more with Richard Branson's take on storytelling as a relationship and trust-building tool. I also teach and use storytelling as a foundation for interviewing and negotiation. Listening to a story is the format in which we all "learn to learn" from the time we are babies.

Not only is the art of storytelling familiar, it brings back warm, comforting memories of sitting on our parents' laps, rocking and listening to their voices share something new, exciting, and engaging. Storytelling and story listening are universal, which is why those techniques work so well in interviewing and negotiations.

Storytelling is at the heart of interviewing. There you are, ready to tell *the* stories of your life so far—in the job interview. If you graduated from a college in which you had to interview to get in, or if you interviewed for an internship that you successfully completed, then you may have already mastered a good deal of the skills necessary to ace an interview for a full time J-O-B. *(See page 37 for a different approach to interviewing: the "informational interview" as a research tool to gain clarity as to the type of career and/or job you may want to pursue.)*

There are some key points to keep in mind when you're sitting before an interviewer.

First, colleges are looking for who you *are*, and whether you have the potential to be communicative, collaborative, and a creative thinker (what I like to call "the 3 Cs"), and a member of the student community. Corporations and organizations, on the other hand, want you to demonstrate your mastery of the 3 Cs in your interview stories. Remember, hiring organizations are either about making money or, in the case of nonprofits, furthering their missions. You can use the stories you tell in your interview to show your potential employer how you can fulfil their company's goals.

For example, Starbucks (a for-profit corporation) wants to make money selling coffee and mugs. UNICEF (a nonprofit organization) wants to further its mission of helping mothers and children in developing countries. For-profits like Starbucks want to know what you can *do with your skills,* how you can contribute to the company's goals and objectives of making money and profits selling coffee and mugs. Nonprofits like UNICEF want to know what you can *do with your skills* to help mothers and children. Let's say you are skilled at website design or digital-content development. These are highly valued skills for either category of employer, because just about every type of organization needs a website, social media, and other digital-media support. Here's the really good news for you. Hiring managers know that you grew up as a "digital native" and likely know a lot more than they do about social media, smartphone habits, and what makes digital content appealing. Leverage this advantage as much as you possibly can by sharing stories about your insights when it comes to everything digital, especially if the job you are interviewing for is a technology-based role.

I recently had an Ivy League university client who was majoring in communications. In her senior year, she was interviewing for digital-content editorial jobs. To demonstrate her ability to analyze and critically think about social-media content, we crafted the following story:

> *When I was a sophomore at an Ivy League university, I was the editor of* Straightline Media, *a digital news source entirely run by students for students. One day, there was a tragic incident in which an apartment building caught on fire. When the news broke, everyone was reading about it online. Every article about the event was purely factual: how the fire happened, who was involved, the aftermath. I wanted* Straightline Media *to contribute to the story with a unique perspective, that of a student. As editor, I knew students value active engagement. I suggested that in place of retelling the factual story about the fire, we inspire action and service within the student community. Therefore, my* Straightline *team created a to-do list suggesting ways students could engage versus passively discussing the fire. On our website, we created a week-long list of daily actions, including donating clothes, toiletries, canned food, and money for survivors of the fire and their families. We provided details on campus locations accepting donations as well. What I am most proud of is that as a result of this fire coverage, students donated and volunteered in record numbers.*

Why is this story so effective? Let's take it apart. This interview story demonstrates a multitude of skills including on-brand, impactful editorial savvy, target-audience recognition, and quick creative and strategic thinking. So, instead of answering the interviewer by simply stating, "My strength is that I am a creative content editor," this story exemplifies that statement. Many people might be uncomfortable with the idea of "bragging" in an interview, but I tell my clients that telling a story in an interview takes the brag out of the answer, making you, the interviewee, a lot more comfortable in your skin!

So, how do you show the interviewer that you're the ideal candidate for the job? Instead of making claims and bragging, you tell them compelling stories about what you have said, thought, and done. Remember those bedtime stories from childhood? Storytelling is familiar, it's engaging, and it follows a methodical thread that can be, dare I say, comforting, or at the very least interesting to the interviewer. People in general like stories that add up and make logical sense. In this instance, using the beginning, middle, and end formula for interview storytelling can help defuse tension during an interview, as well as keep your interviewer engaged. Use this guide (with the *Straightline* news story as the example):

- **(Problem) What problem did you have to solve?** *Report the story in terms of how students use news.*
- **(Action) How did you solve the problem?** *We changed the frame of the story from the facts to ideas for engagement.*
- **(Outcome) What was the result?** *As a result of our*

unique reporting angle, students engaged in record numbers.

To put it simply: interviewing is you telling stories about your experiences through the lens of the job description.

They're *your* stories, so they aren't hard to remember. However, you may be so used to texting, Snapchat, and 280-character tweets that it can be hard to tell a more detailed, specific, word-filled story. Think back to your favorite bedtime story, how it made you feel, how it made sense, and how it came together to explain a concept. My favorite book as a child was *Are You My Mother?* by P. D. Eastman. It's a great example because it's likely a familiar reference to the majority of my readers.

Speak to your interviewer in their reference points, not yours.

If I had said my favorite book was an academic book on communication, you, as my reader, would have no idea what I was talking about. Instead, I referenced a story that you and the majority of my readers know well.

Are You My Mother? has a beginning: Bird hatches, mother bird is MIA, and bird is scared. Middle: Bird is determined to find its mother and ask other animals and inanimate objects if they are its mother. A crane later picks up the bird and places it back in its nest. End: bird reunites with his mother. The story has a logical flow of events. On a deeper level, my telling you that this particular story is my favorite makes even more sense because the interview advice that I offer in this book is my way of mentoring you, a budding professional. In *Are You My Mother?*, the hatchling is seeking a mentor, his mother. Do you see the common thread? It makes perfect sense that my favorite childhood book is about what I do for a living. It's authentic; it rings true. In the same way, your interview answers need to use references familiar to the interviewer, be authentic, have a common thread, add up, and make sense.

A good example of an authentically threaded interview story was when my six-foot-five-inch, redheaded student client was brainstorming answers to a college-leadership scholarship interview question: if you were a tree, what kind of tree would you be? In his research among prior scholarship recipients, the tree question was an FAQ. My student thought back to a family trip to San Francisco and recalled visiting the Redwood Forest. We Googled redwood trees and learned they are the tallest trees. We crafted an answer around redwood trees because he would be taller than all other trees in the forest, and his height would enable him to look out over all the other trees and get "the lay of the land."

Why is this a good answer? The reference point, redwood trees, rings true to who my client is physically—tall and redheaded—and who he is as a leader: someone who looks at the big picture. (Several other interview stories demonstrated his "big picture" leadership style.) The redwood answer added up as a believable metaphor for my client on many levels.

As you tell your story (based on the interviewer's questions), you're also "planting seeds" to prompt the interviewer to ask you specific questions. This intentional "seed-planting" guides the interviewer to the obvious next question, one you already know exactly how to answer. "Seed-planting" at the end of your answer is like a cliffhanger at the end your favorite TV show, the storyline that pulls your binge-watch trigger. I've had clients answer the proverbial "Tell me about yourself" interview question with cliffhanger answers such as: "What I am most proud of is the leprosy research I worked on in Ghana," "I am most proud of the fact that I could deliver excellent emergency medical service on the slopes while I was on skis myself," or "Because of my work, students engaged in victim fire relief in record numbers."

These cliffhanger answers spark interviewer curiosity and make the interviewer want to hear more details about, say, your leprosy-camp volunteer work, being a ski-patrol first responder, or being the editor of a student media source. Wouldn't you yourself want to know more about leprosy or the best ski-patrol rescue story? As a seasoned interviewer myself, I'll tell you, I certainly do!

Another frequently asked interview question that lends itself to a story is "Tell me about a time that you were a leader." One of my clients talked about how he was part of a national venture capital–backed incubator program for high school entrepreneurs, and was placed on a team of introverts. He shared that he himself was an extrovert. He realized as he looked around, he needed to step up and take the lead in unifying the group while dividing and conquering the research and writing. (This is the beginning of his story.) In leading and unifying the group, he organized the research into separate topics, delegated tasks for research, assigned the presentation writing in sections, and answered questions from the venture capitalists (VCs) following the formal presentation. (This is the middle of his story.) The VCs decided not to invest in the company, but informed this young man's team that they thought its presentation and ability to answer questions was the best out of the six high school entrepreneur teams from across the country. (This is the end of his story.)

This is an effective story because it captures much about the person telling it (the interviewee): He's an extrovert; he knows how to assess situations under pressure; he takes charge and also delegates; and he is not afraid to speak in front of intimidating groups. And what's the seed? Well, do you notice any mention of the product the group was pitching? It's not mentioned on purpose. It's the seed to force the next question the interviewer will likely ask: "What was the product or service you were pitching?"

This is where a professional like me comes in to help you identify your potential or existing "transferable" skills that correspond to what a college, grad school, or company/job is looking for in you as an applicant. Like I mentioned before, companies are about making money and nonprofit organizations are about furthering missions. So what can *you*, the interviewee, *do* skill-wise to further those goals? What skill(s) do you have that can contribute to the bottom line or further a mission? Expressing that in a tangible story about your past achievements or experiences powerfully demonstrates to your interviewer that you are a lot more than your résumé. It essentially brings your résumé to life.

How do you do this? I worked with one student to prep him for an interview for a job interview at Burger King corporate in Miami. His résumé indicated his Harvard degree. He'd had a summer internship managing concessions for a minor-league baseball team, and he had worked at a local burger shack during another college summer. (Those past jobs directly "transfer" to a corporate job in the fast-food industry. Do you see the relationship?) His past, relevant job history is why Burger King was interested in interviewing my client. But there was so much more to "bring to life" about his prior experiences in the interview setting. My student understood Burger King's core business—cooking and serving burgers—from the grill up. He also understood inventory management from his minor-league concessions management job. These past experiences were a great interview foundation. However, he needed to go further.

To prep for the interview, I advised him to do his research by visiting and sampling several meal options at a local Burger King the day before the interview and taking a notebook and pen with him. I told him to take note of and write down everything he saw and experienced, from the cleanliness of the bathroom to the speed of service to the quality and taste of the food served. More research. Then, I had him recall and write down everything he did while working at the all-cash burger place in college, from the specific steps he took to open the store, to inventory and ordering cooking ingredients, to cleaning up, to all the details of closing out the cash registers and taking the cash to the bank the next morning.

The next day, when the interviewer asked him, "Why do you want to work here?" he was able to answer with a story like this:

> Since I was a child, I've always loved fast food. In fact, I was in a Burger King yesterday and noticed that though the service was fast once I ordered, the line during the lunch rush was long. It reminded me of my experience working at a burger shack in college. It was a small operation, so I functioned as the supervising manager of a three-person team. I would open the store, make sure the bathroom and floors were clean for customers, cook as well as serve . . . of course I washed my hands in between cleaning the bathroom and cooking the food.

A little appropriate, well-timed humor never hurts in an interview. It says, "I'll be a fun team player!" He ended by saying that when the lunch line was long, he always looked up from the grill to acknowledge waiting customers by saying, "We appreciate your business." This tells the interviewer that he innately understands customer service, a huge component of fast hospitality business.

You get the idea. He showed passion, managerial skills, attention to detail, and that he was responsible. He showed a strong base knowledge of the fast-food industry and attention to the details that make great service and products. His on-paper credentials were good, but I truly believe it was his "day in the life of a burger-shack manager" storytelling that made the interviewer take notice. An Ivy League degree may help you get the interview, but it will not get you an offer.

Detailed, relevant stories that clearly and concisely articulate "transferable" skills are the key to landing job offers for every applicant. I have had many non-Ivy students

A Word and a $hake

land long-shot jobs on Wall Street and in other competitive industries using this core storytelling approach.

Communicating important "transferable" skills is all in the preparation. You *must* do your homework. Study the company website, especially the pages written about the department that you want to work in. After all, that company paid big bucks to come up with a brand statement and articulate brand values. Everything you need to know is all there in black and white in terms of a value system and what they look for in an ideal employee. Just like you research a college for the ideal student character and potential, here you read the About and the In the News company-website tabs. Read posted blogs. If there is a section with photos and bios of key players or your interviewer, study their bios. It is a super easy way to show that you do your homework and arrive (early) prepared, two basic skills that every college and hiring organization wants to see demonstrated. You should also join LinkedIn and read your interviewer's profile on the site.

I can't tell you all of the smart people that I interview who do not do this basic research. I interview young graduates for my SAT/ACT tutoring business. These folks have to be able to score a perfect score on those tests just to land an interview. I am often surprised how many do not visit our website prior to the interview. It makes me hesitant to hire, no matter how good they are. As the interviewer, this research omission makes me question whether, as a tutor in my company, they will do their homework in preparation for tutoring sessions. Do you see how the research skill is transferable? I say visit the interviewing organization's website and study, and reference the website in the interview. Add information to your answers and ask questions in the interview that demonstrate that you spent time reading the site and bios.

Here is an advanced tip: Memorize their bio photos. You never know who will ride the elevator with you up to your interview. It's an opportunity to say, "You are Mr. Jones. I recognize your photo from the website, and I loved your Ted Talk. I'm here interviewing for the marketing analyst position on Tim Smith's team. It's nice to meet you." Extend your hand for a firm handshake. (There's more on handshakes coming right up. Keep reading.) This instance is where the "elevator pitch" got its name.

There are two major things to remember after the actual interview is over. One sounds simple, but it is not: the handshake. (See "Shake It Up" on page 33.) The other is the thank-you note.

Write and email (or snail mail) your thank-you note within twenty-four hours. In your parents' generation, thank-you notes were handwritten, which still is a wonderful personal touch and definitely sets you apart. But, email is absolutely acceptable. Hand delivery, which is totally unnecessary, says "I really want the job."

Essentially, your thank-you email (delivered within twenty-four hours) needs to state the following:

Your email subject line should read, *Thank you for your time.*

> *Dear Mr./Ms. X,*
> *Thank you for the time you spent with me today/yesterday speaking about the X role/job on the*

marketing team. I enjoyed hearing about [name some specific elements of the job and/or company that you learned about in the interview here]. [Another sentence recalling something specific you talked about related to your story/experience]. I would welcome the opportunity to join the Z team.

Thank you again for your time. I look forward to hearing back from you.

Best,
[Your Name]

Boom.

Expect the unexpected when it comes to time. Even if you plan to arrive early, a snafu is always lurking; extra traffic due to a car accident or a stall, or the train gets stuck on the track you have to cross. If it turns out you really will be late for your interview, here is what you do:

Shake It Up

It is the first and last thing you do in a professional interview: shake hands with the interviewer. That initial handshake sets the stage for the interview and can make a big difference in how the interviewer perceives you. You never have another opportunity to make a first impression or an impression last. Those initial and final shakes matter.

Those handshakes must be firm. How firm, you ask? Extend your full hand and shake confidently, like you are grabbing a doorknob and opening a heavy door. The other person, however, should not be in pain. If he or she winces, you know it was too firm. (You'll know if the interviewer winces because you MUST, I repeat MUST, look the other person in the eye while shaking hands.)

Let the other person join your hand, and allow the interviewer to set the shake-squeeze level. And, again, look them in the eye and say confidently, "Thank you. It was so nice to meet you, and I look forward to being in touch." It's as easy as that. Shake it up.

Early Birds

Have you heard the saying "The early bird gets the worm"? Well, I have news for you: the early bird gets the *job*, too. Arriving for an interview at the time of the appointment means you're already late. You should arrive at least fifteen minutes *early*. Like I said earlier, I interview potential tutors for my sister company, Access Test Prep & Tutoring. Nothing makes me happier than an early-arriving interviewee. Early arrival tells me that if I hire them, they will treat our students and their parents with the same respect for their time. Nothing frustrates me more than an interviewee who walks in late and does not apologize or bother to call, text, or email me or my office to alert me of their delay. Late arrival without delay alert makes a negative first impression, and I have yet to even meet the person. Late starts the relationship on shaky footing. Being early means you are respectful of your interviewer's time and the interview process. Remember, until you are the boss, the interviewer's, your boss's, and your client's time is *always* more important than yours.

- Call the interviewer as soon as you realize you will be late. The idea is to demonstrate that you are conscientious and anticipatory, because you are reaching out before the interview start time. If you call at 4:01 p.m., there is already a strike against you. If you call at 4 p.m. on the dot, you are safe, but calling at 3:45 p.m. shouts respect for the interviewer's time.

- To be on the safe side (and continue displaying your level of responsibility and respect for time), also email and text your interviewer as to your expected arrival time (ETA). "I just left you a voicemail letting you know there was a traffic delay (or mistaken address in the case of the Brown interview) and my ETA is 4:15 p.m. I apologize for any inconvenience, and I look forward to meeting you soon." Cover all your communication sources so that if the interviewer only checks one, you have achieved your goal.

What if you are unable to notify your interviewer that you are running late, or you forget to do so? As soon as you arrive, prepare to grovel. "I apologize for my disrespect," you say. "I knew that I was likely going to be late, and I should have called/texted/emailed you. Your time is valuable.

I know that tardiness is unprofessional and assure you that it will never happen again." I can't promise, but this response could save you.

You should also include your cell number.

An email such as this makes it simple for the receiver to forward your message to the person to whom you'd like to be introduced. People worth talking to know that job

Early Birds (cont.)

At times, to ensure that early arrival, I advise clients to visit the interview site the day before, and practice the route there at the time of day you will be traveling on the actual interview day. And, remember your cell phone and phone charger. This might seem like overkill, but it's really not. Here's why.

One of my relatives, who I did not prep, was a lifelong, incredibly talented thespian. She had always wanted to go to Brown University. She was academically qualified, and it was a really good fit for her personality and theatrical career interests. The alumni interviewer emailed and wrote "Meet me at the Starbucks at 4600 Roswell Road at 3:00 p.m." My niece thought she knew which Starbucks was at the 4600 block. It turns out that she was mistaken, and waited and waited at the wrong Starbucks. Yikes! By the time she looked up the address and realized her error, she ended up being thirty minutes late to her Brown interview.

For college, interviews cannot get you in, but being late to one will likely keep you out. She did not get into Brown. She will

> **Early Birds (cont.)**
>
> never know if her late arrival prevented her admission. I do know that it did not help. Later that day, she wrote about her mishap on Facebook. While this story is entertaining social material, colleges and employers often look at your social media.
>
> If for nothing else, colleges look at your social media to gauge your judgment about appropriate posting content. By posting this mishap, you are announcing to all future employers that your attention to detail in critical situations may not be adequate. To be safe, back away from posting anything about interviews. When you are admitted or officially accept the job, feel free to share your good news.

searches are hard and will empathize with your request. Most contacts will appreciate your position and want to help you.

It also pays to talk up your interests and what you are looking for to anyone who will listen. As mentioned in an earlier story, one rising college sophomore had just arrived home for the summer and went with her mother to get a facial. The young woman told the aesthetician about her interest in live-work real estate, and sure enough, the aesthetician had a client who managed a large, local live-work development and put the two in touch! That's how she got her summer internship in real estate.

Note: This client started her search in May and was quite lucky to land an internship, as she was a little late starting. I do advise that you begin searching in January or February for a June internship start date.

When you've made a connection, take full advantage. Be sure to arrive at the meeting with a list of questions already prepared and with a notepad to write down the interviewer's answers. Thank him or her for the time they are spending with you, and express interest in learning more about the industry and job from his or her personal point of view.

Here are my favorite sample questions that work in most any informational interview:

• Tell me about your job from the time you get up until the time that you go to bed. I want to understand what you do every day and the rhythm of your day. What time do you get up? How long is your commute? What do you do during each hour of the day? What is your lunch hour like?

• What motivated you to go into this line of work?

• What was your career path into this job? And how

> **Informational Interviewing**
>
> This chapter deals with you being interviewed, but there's also a reverse interview that you lead: the informational interview. This type of interview is primarily initiated and conducted by *you*, a person who wants to gain more information about a company or industry. You are now interviewing them to find out what exactly people in your targeted industry do all day. Do they sit in a cubicle? Collaborate with clients?
>
> The subject of the interview is a person who works for a company that interests you or within that industry. Hence, the information part of the informational interview.
>
> Let's say you really want to learn more about the digital sports industry. You are open to speaking to any professional in a related industry or company who would make time to speak with you, in their office or a coffee shop, or wherever and whenever is convenient for that person. So, how do you find those professionals? Here's a secret: you know (and are connected) to many more people than you realize.
>
> Make a list of everyone you know that may know someone

Informational Interviewing (cont.)

in that industry. And by "everyone you know," that means your dentist whose son works at CBS Sports; the woman who cuts your hair, who likely has a sports-agent client who might know someone; your sister's best friend's aunt, who used to work for your local CBS affiliate working the camera for local sports coverage, etc. You will be surprised how many people know people. Email, call, or visit each of the people on your list and say something along the lines of this:

I am a University of Georgia graduate seeking informational interviews as I pursue my interest in sports media. [Insert any relevant sports experience you have had, including "I am the current host of UGA football live for all home games."] I understand you have a connection in this field [and list the connection if you know it, such as writing to your dentist that you know has a patient who is a sports agent]. Would you be willing to make an email introduction, and I will follow-up? My résumé is attached. Thank you so much for your help.

did you get this particular position?

- If you were me and looking for a job in this industry, who would you speak to and why? Would you be willing to make an introduction for me?
- What would be your strategy to find a job in this industry? Can you tell me what your job-search roadmap would look like?

When you've asked all your questions (and truly listened to the answers enough to ask some follow-up questions that perhaps were not on your prepared list), thank the person again for his or her time. Follow up with an email thank-you note within twenty-four hours, especially if the interviewer offered or agreed to introduce you to someone else helpful in your job search.

Dear Mr. Jones,

Thank you for your time yesterday. I enjoyed learning more about your career path and the work you do as an agent representing Venus Jones at IMG. As discussed, please forward my attached résumé to your marketing contacts at CBS and CNN Sports. Please CC me on your emails, and I will follow-up immediately with your contacts. Again, thank you for your time.

Best,
Freddie Smith
Cell: 555-555-5555
Email: FSmith202@yahoo.com

This thank-you note says that you will be respectful to their friends in the industry. Learning more about what you do or do not want to do, and securing introductions to those who can help you get to what you want to do are the goals of the informational interview.

One day, you yourself will be the person providing the informational interview!

Chapter 4
The Résumé— Articulating U on Paper

I tell all clients that if you show your résumé to twenty different people, you will get twenty different opinions. The reason is simple: there is no one blueprint for a résumé. Take a look at any template program and you will see what I mean.

Every résumé should, however, include these traits: it should be simple, clear, and concise, including correct tenses, grammar, and spelling. My preferred format is featured in my own résumé on Appendix page 79. My favorite font is Calibri in ten or twelve–point type. For those applying in creative industries like graphic or interior design, or the creative art side of advertising, you can use alternative fonts and design treatments to demonstrate your skill sets and creative thinking. Otherwise, clean and simple is best.

If you are anxious about creating a résumé, you are not alone. In fact, for most of my clients—students, young professionals, and those who are in the middle of their careers—writing a résumé is one of life's most difficult tasks. Why? Writing a résumé is like standing naked in front of a stranger. You're stripped down to your most vulnerable, exposed self. You are "putting yourself out there" on paper. (By the way, I strongly caution you against asking twenty people their opinions of your résumé. It will only overwhelm and freak you out. Find one or two trusted advisors—or hire me!—to guide you.)

Before we talk about what actually goes on your résumé, I must share my own funny but harrowing résumé story as a lesson to all. You may laugh at the idea that back in the mid-1980s, before email, we had to type résumés and cover letters on—*gasp!*—an actual typewriter or clunky "word processor," and print them out, put them in a letter-sized envelope, address the envelope, put some stamps on it, and drop the envelope in a mailbox (those weird blue metal boxes in front of the post office and on some street corners).

So back in 1986, I had been working at a busy and well-respected ad agency before I was unfortunately laid off. (Being laid off, by the way, is different from being fired. When you are laid off, as you one day might experience, you are typically one of the last people hired, and the company is needing to save money so they eliminate positions, including yours.) I was devastated. But thankfully, my mentors helped me update my résumé and wrote me some glowing letters of recommendation to include when I applied for jobs.

I put together nine envelopes for nine different agencies in those standard letter envelopes: my brilliant cover letter, my résumé, and some stellar letters of recommendation. I sealed them and typed the recipients' names and business addresses on the envelopes. I drove them to the mailbox at the post office at about 3:30 p.m., in perfect time for the 5 p.m. mail pick-up.

I dropped them into the box, satisfied and proud. After

A Word and a $hake

I got back into my car, I decided to glance again at my résumé to remind myself to be proud of my accomplishments. Layoffs can be depressing.

And then I saw it and gasped. I found a . . . TYPO. My stomach dropped, like when you begin downhill on a roller coaster.

I was horrified. I knew (as I'm telling you) that a typo on your résumé speaks volumes, and the careless message is *not* the one you want to convey. If you have a typo *anywhere* associated with your job application—on the cover letter or initial email you send, on the résumé itself, on any correspondence with the potential employer—it shouts your lack of attention to detail, and in some ways, it shows disrespect to the company and person considering hiring you. If copy editing is not your thing, have a trusted friend (maybe an English major) or even your parents proofread your résumé and your emails for typos, bad grammar, missing words, etc. before you click "Send."

So back in 1986, what could I do, having realized I was sending those tainted letters? I literally wanted to open the mailbox and crawl inside to retrieve my precious envelopes. But for one, I couldn't fit, and two, it's a federal crime to tamper with mail, even your own. Instead, I did what any self-respecting job applicant would do. I parked myself on the sidewalk next to the mailbox and waited for the mail carrier.

At a few minutes before 5 p.m., he pulled up in his mail truck. I silently prayed he would take pity on me. Maybe he had a daughter my age? I approached him and said, "Sir, I have a problem. I just mailed some résumés to New York City and I found a typo in them. I want to retrieve them from this mailbox. I can tell you the return address with my name and recipient addresses on each of the envelopes before you open the box." He asked for my ID and I showed him my driver's license. He opened the box and a wave of stamped mail came pouring out. Near the top of the pile, I found them: all nine of my envelopes. The kind mailman let me take them. The irony is that he could have lost his job in an effort to help me get mine.

Today, if you find a typo on your "already sent" résumé, simply correct it and immediately email a "typo-free version" to all who received the typo version with this note:

> *Dear Ms. Smith:*
>
> *Attached is a corrected version of my résumé. Unfortunately, I found a typo. Please disregard the résumé that I sent on 1/1/15 and replace it with the attached version. I apologize for any inconvenience, and I hope that you consider my qualifications and my honest mistake.*
>
> *Best,*
> *Elaine Rosenblum*
> *Cell: 888-888-8888*

If I were on the receiving end of the attached email, I would be very impressed by your email, your ability to own your mistake, and your honest willingness to point out your error. It also answers three common interview questions in three short sentences.

1. Tell me about a time you failed.

2. Tell me about a time that you were a leader.
3. Tell me about yourself.

And, your taking ownership of this mistake and correcting it immediately screams HUMILITY and HONESTY, core traits of successful professional "leaders to be." I would very likely interview you based solely on your email and what it says about you.

So, what *should* be in your résumé?

Many people approach writing a résumé by thinking of how they see themselves. But, an effective résumé writer knows that the interview is in the eyes of the beholder, in this case the interviewer (i.e. the potential employer) and his or her needs. The key is to anticipate what the employer wants in an applicant, rather than what *you* are "offering."

Remember from Chapter 3 that businesses and nonprofits are trying to make money and further their missions. So, on your résumé they want to see the skills you have to help them accomplish those goals. This is the angle for your résumé. The interviewer can figure out how to best use your skills, and you can make some suggestions in the actual interview.

Here is a great way a recent graduate and digital-native client shared some of his ideas about how he could help the interviewing company. He was interviewing at a sports-and-entertainment e-commerce ticket-resale site, and had used many of the interviewing company's competitor's e-commerce services. "I spent a lot of time 'clicking around' on your website, and I have bought secondhand tickets from many of your competitors. What

I like about your site is X. *(It is always good to start with a positive.)* I believe that you may be able to increase sales on your site *(share ideas that will help the interviewer reach their goals and make more money)* by doing Y, because it would make obtaining tickets easier for your customers." As a digital native and frequent user of these services, you might have customer insight that the interviewers missed. If nothing else, your interviewer will appreciate your problem-solving approach to their business.

You may see some résumés with an "objective" at the top, which states what type of job you are looking for. I advise writing more of a short profile, a snapshot of who you are. It's like an Instagram photo that summarizes you or your experience in a snapshot. A good example of a recent graduate résumé profile might read like this: "Trilingual sports marketing professional with international/domestic beverage experience, including at the Olympics, golf, cycling, football, and baseball events across multiple venues."

I interview potential tutors every week for my other business, Access Test Prep & Tutoring. I am frequently switching gears from working with a client on interview prep to walking directly into an interview with a potential tutor. Résumé profiles help me refresh my memory in a matter of seconds. Do interviewers a favor and have a profile at the top of your résumé. If an interviewer reads nothing else, he or she will have good idea of YOU in one or two sentences.

When you are a recent graduate starting your professional career, the best type of résumé is a chronological one: a clear, simple, bullet-pointed list of the organizations, your internship or job title, what you did in that role, how you accomplished it, and what the results were (see examples of résumé entries on Appendix page 82). Bullet points should begin with action verbs, such as "created," "developed," "managed," and "supported."

For example, I've mentioned my student client who worked for an all-cash burger joint one summer. In his résumé description of his job at the burger shack, he wrote:

- "Made and served burgers"
- "Worked as a cashier"

I encouraged him to include more professional verbs. I asked him, "So, what did you actually *do*?" We revised his résumé to include bullets with more detailed and professional words, such as:

- "Entrusted to cash out register, which included handling $3,000 per day and depositing it into the company's bank account"
- "Managed a team of three, including supervising service, opening, and closing the restaurant"

Using these *professional organizational* terms, as well as adding the specific amounts of money he was in charge of, tells the résumé reader, "My employer trusted me with her money and bank account, as well as to manage others in a service role."

Creating a strong résumé means taking the personal

out of it. Note that the bullets above are written objectively. Neither bullet states "I was entrusted" or "I managed." Remember, your résumé really has little to do with you as a person and everything to do with what skills you have that can contribute to the bottom line or accomplishing the mission of XYZ organization. Think of your résumé as a proposal to help an organization further its goals. This will help you feel less vulnerable and more focused. So, keep your clothes on. And remember: NO TYPOS.

Chapter 5
Speaking the Language of Negotiation

If you nailed the résumé and job interviews, I'm 99 percent sure that if you want one, you will receive a job offer. Just keep applying, networking, and interviewing until you get an offer. If you are getting second and third interviews, that means your interviewing skills are serving you. If you are getting cut off after first interviews, it's time to call me or review and role play your interview answers with a mentor or trusted advisor.

If you get an offer, you can relax; you are in the driver's seat. But, you are not quite finished with the deal. Bask in that pride for just a minute . . . then turn your attention to the art of salary negotiation. You might be hesitant to consider this; after all, this is your first real job! However, if you skip this step and accept the job on the spot, you are leaving good money on the table.

Just what is salary negotiation, exactly? Essentially, negotiating means advocating for yourself to get the best possible salary, benefits, and all-around "package." You have proven that you are valuable to the company. Can they now prove that they are worth it to *you*?

Negotiation skills are essential life skills, so it's never too early to learn and practice them. I teach a model called collaborative salary negotiation, which is the idea that a

49

successful outcome serves both parties' needs, and comes from shifting away from defensive and extreme wording toward an offensive partnership mindset and collaborative language.

For example, though this potential employer has offered the job that you want, you do have a "dog in this fight" if you see the company as a partner rather than an adversary who is out to take advantage of you, which can make you defensive. So, using "we" and asking open-ended questions to gain information will help you set the tone of the negotiated conversation. Your mindset, your word choice, and your ability to listen are the keys to the practice of collaborative salary negotiation.

Before you effectively negotiate a counteroffer, you need to have all the information available to you: salary, benefits package (paid time off, health insurance, etc.), any stock options or other financial information the company is offering you, and some information about the company culture/perks. Is there, for example, a free gym on site, extra time off for volunteer opportunities, or tuition reimbursement? Ask for all the salary and benefits information in writing. Lay it all out on a table somewhere quiet, enlist a trusted mentor, friend, or parent, and review your options.

Keep in mind that whatever information provided is just the organization's first "offer." When companies make a job offer, they typically low-ball you, because they anticipate a salary negotiation. So, when you get the offer, thank the employer for the opportunity and say, "I need a few days to research and review the details of the offer." Note: by "a few days," you mean three days maximum.

I can't stress enough that if you don't ask for more, you are leaving good money on the table. In twenty years, I have never seen or heard of an employer retracting the offer or lowering the initial offer because a potential employee counteroffered. To create a fair counteroffer, do some research on the range of pay rates in the industry for the geographic area where you will be based. Employers in cities such as New York, Los Angeles, and San Francisco frequently compensate for higher costs of living.

After digesting the initial offer, decide what you want: the amount that is either the initial offer or only a bit higher, or your "walk away," an amount so low that you are unwilling to accept the job. Start by asking the recruiter or hiring manager, "Is that salary flexible or negotiable?" The company representative may falter, but even if he or she says the salary is firm, still tell them you need some time to think. Even if you do not have multiple offers, you still need to weigh these factors to determine if there is, in fact, "wiggle room" on the initial offer.

For example, one twenty-three-year-old client was negotiating for her first salary in a TV/movie talent agency. She wanted to counter the initial offer because she could stay on her parents' insurance for another three years. She wanted the organization's contribution to her health insurance to be lumped into her base salary instead. She asked, and her new employer happily obliged. She added $5,000 to her base salary with that one question. This is salary negotiation.

Yes, you may be young, and this may be your first job out of college or grad school. You may feel counteroffers and negotiations sound "pushy," or worry that you are being "too difficult." You are mistaken. If you read nothing else in this book, read this: **I am absolutely, unequivocally positive that an employer who has extended you an offer will actually respect you more if you negotiate your initial salary offer than if you do not. (Just do so collaboratively.) I feel confident no employer will revoke an offer. You have nothing to lose.**

Most budding professionals are so relieved to have a job that they mistakenly accept and start working. Employers are impressed when you negotiate because it means that you will "transfer" those negotiation skills to your new job and negotiate hard in your role on behalf of the organization.

Research shows that it is frequently women who feel "negotiation shy," but my male clients fall into this trap, too. Ignore that voice that insists you are being confrontational or asking too much when you negotiate. You are being quite the opposite, actually: you are displaying real confidence and professionalism. At offer, you gain the advantage. Understand your worth and do your research. Glassdoor.com is a great source for this research.

Here is a story from *Women Don't Ask: The High Cost of Avoiding Negotiation—and Positive Strategies for Change* by Babcock and Laschever. Although the book is aimed at women, it applies to men, too. It will light a fire under you when it comes to negotiation. Consider an applicant, Toni, who did not initiate a salary negotiation when she received a first job offer, which was $25,000 at age twenty-two. She took the offer and began working. If she had asked for just $5,000 more, and she continued investing the incremental money that she continued to negotiate for in all future salary negotiations until she was sixty-five, she would have almost $800,000. You simply cannot afford—literally—to ignore the opportunity to negotiate, even for small incremental amounts, from that first job offer through retirement, because over time the money adds up.

Another client of mine, a male who was graduating from a prestigious MBA program, had received an offer from a large global airline to work on its frequent-flyer program. He loved travel, so he was thrilled about the job offer. The airline offered him a $150,000 base salary. I told him to ask for more using this language:

> *Thank you. I appreciate the offer and I am excited. I need to think about the offer, and I believe that it's a start. In the interim, would you please provide the offer in writing to me and include a copy of the benefits book and the employee handbook so that I may consider all the information included in the offer?*

When you return to the company with your counteroffer, be sure to use that collaborative language. Remind them how happy and appreciative you are that they offered you a position. Explain that you did some research on salaries in the industry, the city in which you will work, and cost of living in the area in which you would be working.

"I appreciate your initial offer of X. To be honest, I was expecting a higher starting salary, given my experience (be specific)" and/or "Industry standards indicate a salary range of X to X for this job in [city]. As such, would we be able to have me start at X?"

Pause and let the employer respond.

In my MBA client's case, the airline came back with $20k more. So had he NOT negotiated, he would have left $20K on the table. That's not chump change!

If the employer will not budge on salary, bring new variables to the negotiating table. Ask, "Is there another way that you have added to a potential employee's total package that has created value other than salary?"

Here is a list of examples that you may want to suggest:

- Signing bonus or yearly bonus
- Higher commission structure
- Tuition assistance
- Equipment such as cell phone, car, parking, computer, home office
- Paying more of monthly health-insurance premiums
- Moving up the date healthcare coverage takes effect

Hopefully, your new employer will add some value in one or more of the above areas. If not, ask, "Is there another way that I have not yet suggested that you have added to a potential employee's total package that has created value other than salary?" Pushing hard on adding value ensures that you cover all of your bases, leave no stones unturned, and leave no money on the table. The idea here is to negotiate hard on the variables and to be polite to the people (i.e. the hiring managers). And remember: If you never ask, you will never get.

Chapter 6
Are You My Mentor?—Knowing People Who Know

You have likely heard the word "mentor" batted around in various forms like "role model," "advisor," and "guru." A mentor is all of these things, and it's good to have one.

A mentor, someone who is experienced and already doing what you professionally want to do, or who is well-versed in the professional world, can set you on the path to success. This person can review your résumé, help with job-interview prep, offer "insider" tips and insights into various industry sectors, serve as a reference, make introductions, and act as a sounding board and support system as you carve out your career. After all, success is not a straight-line trajectory. It's more of a jagged line, like an EKG readout. A mentor can help stabilize that path.

To truly benefit from mentorship, it is a good idea to "formalize" your relationship by straight-out asking someone to be your mentor. Likely, the person will be flattered.

Make a point of checking in regularly. I suggest having a monthly date to meet for coffee, which is quick and inexpensive. Agree to meet the first Monday morning of every month at 8:00 a.m. at the same Starbucks. It will become a ritual. Set up a time to video chat, or meet your mentor before you have an important work meeting or presentation. Perhaps you want to practice and get your mentor's feedback on your point of view or thinking about a problem. The most important way to utilize a mentor is to ask for pointers on how to make the most of opportunities to impress your boss and team.

Seasoned professionals do this consistently, and mentoring plays a huge role in their success. I only send important letters or give presentations after a trusted friend or mentor has reviewed and edited for typos and logic. And, as a mentor, I frequently edit and provide feedback on documents for my clients. It's simply too hard to spot errors and edit your own work. Why do you think great writers all have editors?

Having a mentor that is unassociated with your organization is actually better. It takes office politics off the table and makes it likely that you can trust your mentor's opinion 100 percent. Most successful people agree that if it were not for their mentor's guidance, their success would have been far less likely.

Established professionals find it rewarding to assist younger people in business coming up the ranks. Trust me, they vividly remember when they were starting out. All you have to say is "I want to learn from your expertise." In this case, flattery will take you far!

My client Chloe just graduated from the University of Georgia. She has gotten multiple second and third interviews in many organizations. She frequently worried about which job she would take. As her mentor, I assured her that her concerns were wasted energy. I advised making interviewing a game and challenging herself to get as many offers as possible. Then she would have all the required information to compare a list of pros and cons, such as cities, salaries, industries, and career-path quality. She has since accepted a job at a large Chicago consulting firm.

Before meeting with your mentor, write down questions you have about:

- Business and organizational strategies
- How to work through problems and conflicts to get promoted
- How to know when (and how) to ask for a raise
- How to identify and ask for feedback on skill areas that need improvement
- How to know when it's time to seek a job elsewhere

Most importantly, mentors can make introductions to other professionals. As a mentor to many, I do not have all the answers, but I frequently know someone who does. The beauty of mentors is that they know people who know. Good questions to ask your mentor are:

- What would you choose to do differently if you could go back to the start of your career?
- What do you wish you knew when you were at my professional level?

A mentor can help you view your career in an active, "big picture" way, rather than simply going to work and doing your job. Mentors have perspective and can identify opportunities and priorities. Like Chloe, young professionals sweat stuff that is wasted energy. It's great to have a mentor reassuringly say, "That's nothing to worry about."

Just this week, I have heard of two college seniors that were asked for their follow-up thoughts after job and informational interviews at media companies. Do not underestimate or ignore this compliment and enormous opportunity to "show what you know." In the digital economy, those doing the hiring know that YOU, a digital native, know more about millennial digital mindset and habits than they do. That's extremely valuable information and why they want your opinion and insight. Use the opportunity. Write an email thanking the interviewer for their time and alerting them that you will be sending your proposed suggestions on updating the newsletter format to appeal to millennial readers and will deliver by May 15, 2017. Then, sit down and write out a bullet point PowerPoint. Then, ask a trusted advisor to review it and submit it.

My client Chloe, the University of Georgia graduate, had a successful interview with the chief marketing officer (CMO) of a large publishing company. The CMO sent Chloe a link to a newsletter that needed increased millennial readership. The interviewer was testing Chloe's initiative to set herself apart. It was an opportunity for Chloe to create a presentation and give recommendations to improve the newsletter based on her previous experience as editor of a digital, student-run newspaper and from a digital native's point of view. He asked her because she is closer than the CMO to a millennial age, she was an editor of a student newspaper targeted at young readers, and she grew up with technology. Chloe wrote a Google Slides deck and smartly had me read it before she submitted. Chloe took initiative, sought mentor feedback, and landed the job.

Mentors see opportunities that might be in your blind spot, and encourage key projects or additional work that will serve you and get you noticed and promoted. It's up to you to take initiative, and your mentor can assist you in the writing, language, and strategy to support your effort.

So, how do you find a mentor? Finding the right mentor is not random.

A mentor should be someone you admire who can teach you. Ideally, your mentor is working in an industry in which you are seeking employment or is a seasoned professional. For example, I have some friends whose son launched a start-up. His father, a successful business owner, advised him regularly. Sometimes a fresh set of eyes and ears can be invaluable. In a brief social conversation, the son listened to one of my passing suggestions regarding his LinkedIn profile. He rewrote it, and then wisely sent it to me for more feedback. This small advice-giving and advice-seeking interaction soon morphed into a mentor-mentee relationship. So, if someone with more professional experience gives you valuable advice, it is a clue that you are dealing with a potential mentor. Take note, and propose the idea of testing out a more formal mentoring relationship. Do work your social connections. There is a great deal of seasoned, professional brain power out there for the taking. Try someone who has about a decade's worth of experience on you, someone who can look back and share insight.

Here is a sample email to a prospective mentor:

> *Dear Ms. Smith,*
> *I am looking for a mentor to guide me through my career in [x industry]. I would welcome the opportunity to buy you coffee and discuss how we might work together. What are convenient days and times that you are available either before 8 a.m. or after 6 p.m.?*

If it ends up being a productive meeting, at the end of the meeting ask, "Will you be my mentor?" and agree to a meeting schedule right then, i.e. the first Monday of every month, 8 a.m. at Starbucks at Lenox Mall. Or, write a thank-you email within twenty-four hours. Here is a sample email thank-you note to a prospective mentor:

> *Thank you for meeting with me yesterday. I enjoyed learning more about your career path. I'd like to make this a more formal mentor relationship, so may I reach out to you periodically when I need guidance in my job and career?*

Intraorganizational mentorships, the kind where your mentor works in your own company, can have an upside and a downside. The upside is that they understand your company intimately and can "show you the ropes." However, the downside is that person is part of the company, too, and therefore may not be objective or have your best interests as a priority. He or she may think more about his or her loyalty to the business itself.

It is helpful to have a mentor-type relationship with

someone in your company mainly to get you smart on the organizational politics, but I suggest tapping someone outside of your company for a more formal relationship. If the outside mentor is good, she can strategize with you about who on the inside to ask specific questions so that you get the political insight that you need, as well as guide you about advancing your own career and capitalizing on *your* skills and strengths.

As a young professional, my mentor was a man named Barry. We met when I was a student at The University of Texas at Austin. At the time, he was president of a large advertising agency in the South. I was an advertising-and-communications major, and could not pass up the opportunity to ask him point blank, "How am I going to get a job in advertising?" Barry was both amused by and impressed with my question. Barry agreed to advise me, and I needed it. (By the way, this is mentorship.) It was the early 1980s. There was an oil crisis in Texas, which put the state economy in a slump, making entry-level advertising jobs hard to land. Barry told me he would hire me in a minute. Unfortunately for me, Barry's agency was in Houston and I wanted to be in Dallas. He said, "The Dallas job market has ad jobs with national clients," meaning a broader career path for me. It turned out that Barry was right on the money.

Although I was graduating with a high GPA from The University of Texas at Austin, one of the country's prized advertising and communications colleges, it was still extremely competitive and difficult to get an entry-level ad agency job in 1985 Dallas, Texas. I ended up doing several informational interviews, and many agencies liked my résumé and internships . . . but the Texas economy was in the toilet.

I did an informational interview at the agency that developed advertising for a low-cost, then-cutting-edge (now defunct) airline brand called Braniff. Barry urged me to write the head of account management, a man named Bob Mook, and explain why I wanted to work at this agency. (There was no email back then. This was snail mail!) When I did not hear back after several weeks, Barry encouraged me to make follow-up calls. I now call this "polite persistence," and it paid off. Mr. Mook eventually called me back. Through my tenacity, I was subtly showing Mr. Mook my work ethic, how I would professionally treat his clients, and that I was unafraid of taking a risk. When he asked me to come in for another interview, I again consulted with mentor Barry, who coached me on my interview skills (similarly to how this book is coaching *you*). I was able to sell myself to Mr. Mook as a promising young marketer and creative problem solver.

Mr. Mook wanted to hire me, but he didn't have the money to pay me. When I got home, I was so disappointed and immediately called Barry. Barry advised me to write Mr. Mook a thank-you note proposing that I come work for his agency for a specific amount of time as an unpaid intern. Although I would not be paid, Barry reasoned, I was not being paid to *not* work, either. Between not working and working for free, the unpaid job was the better option. An internship provided me the opportunity to further prove myself as an exemplary potential employee; I got hands-on work experience at a well-respected agency;

and I could add the experience as another "experience" entry on my résumé. Plus, it got me out of bed and off the couch, helping me gain some much-needed self-respect. Thanks to my mentor, I seized an opportunity that I would have otherwise blindly missed.

On the night before my first day of the two-month internship, my mentor Barry gave me the following piece of business advice, which I still consider the single best professional advice I have ever gotten. He said, "Elaine, if you don't f— up twice a day, you are not working hard enough." I heed this advice even today, because it reminds me to give myself (and others) permission to make two mistakes a day. I often make many more, as do most humans, but remembering this gives me the enduring confidence to recover from and own my mishaps and right the wrong. Owning and correcting the impact of your mistakes earns you respect (see typo discussion in Chapter 4, page 43).

On my first day working for Mr. Mook at the agency, I garnered some additional respect when I looked him straight in the eye and said, "I am going to work so hard that I will embarrass you into paying me." Three weeks later, I had a salary, benefits, and a plumb entry-level account-management position at one of the most respected advertising agencies in the South—on a national account, Braniff Airlines, to boot. It could not get better than that . . . unless I was working at a big advertising agency in New York City.

Guess what? Eighteen months later, I was.

PS: Thank you, Barry, for your encouragement, wisdom, and advice. Thank you, Bob, for believing in me and giving me the opportunity to work so hard that I embarrassed you into paying me what I deserved. Both of you were my first professional mentors, and the inspiration and wisdom that you imparted is in part this book and the reason for my business, ProForm U.

Chapter 7
Speaking Up and Out

SOCIAL MEDIA AND INTERVIEWING

I would be remiss if I did not mention social media in terms of interviewing. Colleges, universities, and potential employers check what you write and photos posted on your social-media pages. I urge all of my students and clients to be very thoughtful and careful about posting content.

If you need proof of why, look no further than this headline by Hannah Natanson in the *Harvard Crimson*: "Harvard Rescinds Acceptances for At Least Ten Students for Obscene Memes." The article also cited Kaplan Test Prep's survey of more than 350 college admissions officers.

- 35 percent of admissions officers check social media like Facebook, Twitter, and Instagram to learn more about applicants[2]
- Of those surveyed, 44 percent said what they found had a *negative impact* on applicants[3]

---

[2] Darian Somers, "Do Colleges Look at Your Social Media Accounts?" *U.S. News & World Report*, February 10, 2017, https://www.usnews.com/education/best-colleges/articles/2017-02-10/colleges-really-are-looking-at-your-social-media-accounts.

[3] Hannah Natanson, "Harvard Rescinds Acceptances for At Least Ten Students for Obscene Memes," *The Harvard Crimson*, June 5, 2017,

According to a 2016 Harris Poll conducted for CareerBuilder, the number of employers using social media to screen candidates has increased 500 percent over the last decade.[4]

- 70 percent of employers use social-networking sites to research job candidates, up from 60 percent in 2016
- 54 percent have declined to hire an applicant based on their social media content
- 33 percent of employers have found content online that has caused them to reprimand or FIRE an employee

SPEAKING UP

No matter how many good mentors you have, you must speak up when your mentor is not around. That means if you have a thought in a meeting or when socializing with teammates, and you believe it adds value, share it. It is a way for you to gain recognition, respect, credibility, and to be noticed for your contributions. If speaking

---

https://www.thecrimson.com/article/2017/6/5/2021-offers-rescinded-memes/.
4 "Number of Employers Using Social Media to Screen Candidates at All-Time High, Finds Latest CareerBuilder Study," CareerBuilder, June 15, 2017,
http://press.careerbuilder.com/2017-06-15-Number-of-Employers-Using-Social-Media-to-Screen-Candidates-at-All-Time-High-Finds-Latest-CareerBuilder-Study.

up seems too risky, after the meeting or conversation, approach your boss or a teammate one-on-one and say, "I was thinking about today's meeting and I had a thought. I want to know what you think of solving the problem by doing X."

This conversation is far less risky, and proposing your theory or idea as a question rather than a statement gives your boss or teammate a chance to tell you why your idea may be good or somewhat good but has some flaws. If you do not understand the gaps in your thinking, ask, "Can you explain to me why this part of my thinking has gaps?"

If asking for clarification seems too risky, you are still ahead by showing your boss or teammate that you are thinking about the organization's problems and issues. Repeat the story to your mentor, and hopefully he or she will be able to explain the pros and cons of your thinking. Remember, all organizations are just a bundle of problems and issues waiting for good solutions. Bosses sleep better when they know that you are thinking about how to solve these problems, and mentors enjoy helping you brainstorm potential solutions.

SPEAKING OUT

Make it a habit to be on the lookout to speak out. Recognize opportunities in the interviewing process to show your thinking. Here's why . . .

In today's knowledge economy, the name of the game is disruption and interruption. Hiring managers know that you are a digital native, meaning you grew up immersed in technology. They know that you understand—better than they do—how to navigate technology, and how you and your generation prefer to engage. Hiring managers want you to speak out and tell them what and how you think.

Many interviewers are interested in hiring you to help increase their millennial audience/users. If they interview and like you, they may end by saying something like, "We are working on this new newsletter, and I would like to hear your thoughts on it. I will send you a link." Do *not* ignore this. It's a piece of bait and a huge opportunity in disguise. Two of my student clients were challenged in this manner, one at a large magazine publisher and one at a documentary-film production company. I encouraged both to bite. The one who did got a job. The one who did not, well, you can guess what happened. Speak out, because you have absolutely nothing to lose and perhaps a job offer to gain. Here's what to say in response to the bait or floated challenge:

> *I would welcome the opportunity to share my thinking on the content, ease of use, and design of the newsletter site. I will send you a proposal by end of day May 1 (two or three days later).*

I suggest writing a Google Slides or PowerPoint deck outlining your thinking and submitting it by 5 p.m. no later than day three. Submitting on or before deadline builds trust and demonstrates accountability, which are key skills for building relationships and demonstrating professionalism. Have a mentor or trusted advisor read the deck before you submit it to ensure the proposals are logical, flow, and are free from typos.

Do not let this overwhelm you. It does not have to be long or perfect, as you are not yet an expert in their field. The deck just needs to be well thought out and perhaps provide insights into a digital native perspective.

SPEAKING TOWARD SUCCESS

We live and work in a knowledge economy, meaning everything we need to know can be found on a computer. What's valued by hiring organizations is not what you know, but what you can do with what you can find. That means you need to be able to communicate and collaborate with others in order to innovate or disrupt. Communicating and collaborating toward innovation requires articulation, or skillfully speaking and writing with words.

I spend a lot of time guiding budding, young, and seasoned professionals about how they speak and write. Why? Because all of us are influenced by our world of intersecting cultural variables, including information overload, extreme beliefs, values, rhetoric, language, "dissing," and omitted words.

We text-abbreviate and often use symbols to replace entire paragraphs of words. I get the convenience and speed gratification, but in the professional world, where disrupting and innovating are the goal, some very important details get lost in the conversion from full words to symbols. Text code and symbols are a recipe for miscommunication and are counter to the collaboration that creates innovation, the secret that speaks to success in the knowledge economy.

Chapter 8
Cuz, Like, Do I Have to Use SAT Words?

I vividly remember stuttering to get the words out in the first months of my first full-time job. I would arrive in my apartment at night and my brain would literally hurt. Entering a professional setting on a full-time basis includes mastering a new vocabulary and language: professional speak. Workers immersed in the professional world speak professionally on autopilot, professional to professional. Even more challenging is that each industry has a lingo, which you will innately learn, but it does cause some initial confusion. Entering the workspace full time is like traveling to a country where you don't fully speak the language. Be patient; there is a learning curve.

Like I said, careers are not straight-line upward trajectories. While there will be ups and downs (everyone has them), there is language that can ensure your line of progression continues in a positive direction. It starts with your words.

The most frequent feedback I give to students and clients is to add "be" before "cuz" and to refrain from overusing the "like" word. We live in a culture where lines of appropriate behavior are blurred, our words are slurred, and some words are being replaced by smiley-face emojis.

One day soon you will be the boss and make the rules.

For now, my generation makes the rules, and I want you to know our standards. In a word, ARTICULATE. It's an adjective and a verb. We want you to "be articulate," adjective, and "to articulate," verb.

What does that mean exactly?

How you communicate reflects on you, and your word choice is the litmus test. I use my articulation strategy to help students and clients land college seats, scholarships, internships, jobs, and promotions to the C-suite. It works 98 percent of the time.

Need proof? My clients have landed in the Ivy League, White House, Wall Street, Silicon Valley, big-box retail, NYC fashion houses, and in Hollywood, to name a few. Your listener may not be able to put their finger on why they are impressed by you, but they will know that you are speaking their language. This will serve your movement up.

Although culture has relaxed and jeans are appropriate in some workplaces, employers now value refined communication skills more than ever. In a knowledge economy, where creativity, collaboration, and disruption are the goals, miscommunication is the enemy and success resides in your word choice. In your written and verbal communications, say exactly what you mean rather than giving half-baked efforts to state your point of view.

I am frequently asked if one needs to use SAT words in interviews and other professional communications. My answer is always a firm NO! The smartest, most successful people I know do not use big words. They use very specific language to communicate ideas and positions as briefly as possible.

A Word and a $hake

I have tried to model brief clarity and specific communication throughout this book. Feel free to use any phrasing, framing, or words. If you struggle with speaking or writing, enlist a mentor, professional, parent, English major, or me to give you feedback and edit your most important workplace communications and general speaking style. Review what you want to say or write with these trusted advisors until it becomes part of your vocabulary. I teach people this transition from "text, social speak" to "professional speak" almost daily, and after a few months they can switch voices without thinking.

Since 4K, my son has attended the Atlanta International School, which is a dual-language immersion IB school. One key strategy the school uses to speed fluency is to have two distinct classrooms, English and Spanish. So, too, when you are at work, use your professional voice and vocabulary, and when texting with friends use your text, social speak. And remember, you are only as good as your word.

Onward and upward, friends.

Appendix

Sample Cover Letter

Ken Smith
Ken.Smith@tufts.edu
(c) 928-555-5555

JPMorgan Chase & Co.
270 Park Avenue
New York, NY 10172

Dear Hiring Manager,

As a Tufts University political science and economics major with a 3.87 GPA, I have developed a strong interest in the intersection of government regulations and financial systems. I am eager to apply my classroom knowledge and experiences as a Compliance Summer Analyst at JPMorgan Chase & Co.

As a Tufts Audit and Management Advisory Services intern, I researched and evaluated departmental compliance issues including financial risks, federal regulations, and internal controls. Specifically, in an Athletics Department audit, I pinpointed the need for student employment to comply with Massachusetts regulations regarding background checks.

Most recently, I worked in the office of US Senator Cory Booker. I collaborated with the policy team to create a report outlining the impact of increases in the federal minimum wage on constituents and New Jersey corporations. I have also worked in a variety of roles that required attention to detail and effective interpersonal and written communication skills, including a public legal-defense organization, an on-campus business, and with elected officials. While working in a

Elaine Rosenblum, JD

state senator's office in Lower Manhattan, I wrote a thirty-page policy report that examined the deficient conditions in the district's subway stations, including potential regulatory reforms.

Given my academic record, I hope to utilize my analytical, communication, leadership, and organizational skills as a Summer Analyst in the JPMorgan Compliance Department. I hope that you will consider my qualifications and experience favorably.

Sincerely,

Ken Smith
Ken.Smith@tufts.edu
(c) 928-555-5555

Elaine Rosenblum Résumé

Elaine Susan Rosenblum, JD
80 West Wieuca Rd. NE, Suite 120
Atlanta, GA 30342
404-303-1118
Elaine@ProFormU.com
ProFormU.com

PROFILE

Seasoned entrepreneur, communications expert, attorney, mentor, and teacher; expertise in mediation, collaborative negotiation, conflict management, marketing, creative problem solving, and management within large organizations.

PROFORM U, Atlanta, GA and New York, NY
Principal/Founder (2014–Present)
- Founder of mentoring/communications consulting firm; developed unique communication model combining mediation, collaborative negotiation, and marketing techniques to refine communication skills among students and professionals, from middle school students to C-suite executives
- Teach/mentor students and professionals at all levels to articulate, write, collaborate, and negotiate across a myriad of disciplines and professions, including résumé development, admissions, internship and job interviews (private, college, graduate, medical, dental schools, medical residency, banking, consulting, corporate, and non-profit organizations), negotiation, presentation, conflict resolution, creative problem solving, and management skills

ACCESS TEST PREP & TUTORING, Atlanta, GA
Cofounder (2006–Present)
- Cofounded comprehensive one-on-one tutoring organization for standardized tests, academics, and professional skills across forty tests and academic subjects including SAT, SAT II, ACT, AP, SSAT, ICEE, MCAT, LSAT, GMAT, and GRE
- Provide one-on-one tutoring featuring ProForm U résumé, interview, collaborative negotiation, and verbal and written articulation skills to middle, high school, college, and post-graduate students seeking admissions, internships, and jobs

COURAGEOUS CONVERSATION, New York, NY and Atlanta, GA
President/Founder (2001–Present)
- Founder of conflict-management consulting firm providing consulting engagements, coaching for individuals/teams, training seminars, and key notes for groups
- Conduct mediations facilitating collaborative discussion between a company and clients, trade/joint venture partners, vendors and individuals, teams, and divisions working within an intracompany or interorganizational paradigm

NEW YORK UNIVERSITY; THE CITY UNIVERSITY OF NEW YORK, BARUCH COLLEGE; AND COLUMBIA UNIVERSITY, New York, NY
Assistant Adjunct Professor (2003–2005)
- Taught attorneys/corporate executives a ten-week, collaborative negotiation course at NYU's Conflict and Dispute Resolution program
- Taught introductory and advanced collaborative negotiation and conflict resolution in an eight-week class as part of Baruch College Continuing and Professional Studies program
- Taught Baruch College undergraduate business law course
- Co-instructed Columbia University Leadership in Law summer program

CORPORATE MARKETING/ADVERTISING
RAPP COLLINS WORLDWIDE
TIME, INC.
J. WALTER THOMPSON, INC.
McCANN-ERICKSON WORLDWIDE
SAATCHI & SAATCHI WORLDWIDE, New York, NY
Consultant/Management Representative (1986–1998 and 2000–2001)

Client roster: **Delta, Northwest, Lufthansa, and Braniff Airlines; Mercedes-Benz USA; Bank One/First USA; The Discovery Channel; Nestlé Beverage Company; Nabisco; Cunard Cruise Lines, Hotels, and Resorts;** *Entertainment Weekly, Fortune, Life, Money, People, Sports Illustrated,* **and** *Time* **magazines**

- Supervised daily operations managing multilevel teams and collaborating across agency support disciplines and 20+ client contacts, including cross-divisional partnering within client organizations
- Oversaw allocation/creative execution of multimedia client campaigns and advertising budgets up to $70M; responsible for yearly account profit/loss

EDUCATION

Harvard Law School, Advanced Negotiation Training for Lawyers
J.D., Benjamin N. Cardozo School of Law, New York, NY, Admitted to New York State Bar
B.S., Advertising, School of Communications, University of Texas, Austin, TX

Sample Achievement Résumé

Ken Smith

928-346-3343 | Ken.Smith@tufts.edu

EDUCATION
Tufts University — Medford, MA
Bachelor of Arts in Political Science; Minor in Economics — August 2014 – May 2019
- GPA: 3.87/4.00; Relevant Coursework: Financial Accounting & Corporate Finance, Industrial Organization, Intermediate Microeconomic Theory, Intermediate Macroeconomic Theory, Political Foundations of Economic Prosperity, Social Marketing
- Honors/Awards: Published in the *Butler Journal of Undergraduate Research*, elected to *Honos Civicus* (Tufts Civic Honor Society) and *Pi Sigma Alpha* (Political Science Honor Society), achieved Deans List all semesters

WORK EXPERIENCE
Barclays Investment Bank — New York, NY
Summer Compliance Analyst — June 2017 – August 2017
- Reported to the Americas Head of Surveillance and assisted with Trade, Control Room, and Special Situations Surveillance
- Executed daily surveillance on Equity Research desks to keep firm's information barriers intact and prevent insider trading
- Created new electronic database to increase productivity of 100 daily Trade Surveillance models
- Presented a pro/con analysis of the Financial Choice Act to 90 employees as part of a 3-member summer analyst team

ProForm U, LLC. — Medford, MA & Atlanta, GA
Marketing Director, On-Campus Pilot Program — December 2017 – Present
- Initiated entrepreneurial partnership for scalable professional interview prep service; design and oversee marketing for Tufts campus test of on-campus interview prep service; acquired 15 Tufts student/clients and anticipate scaled expansion to additional campuses

Tufts University Audit & Management Advisory Services — Medford, MA
Audit Intern — September 2016 – May 2017
- Conducted operational and financial audits of university departments to assess compliance with financial laws, federal research regulations, and internal controls; researched, analyzed and generated responses to enact compliance with Senior Auditors

Office of US Senator Cory Booker — Newark, NJ
District Office Intern — January 2016 – May 2016
- Assisted constituents in navigating federal government agencies and conducted community outreach efforts throughout the state
- Researched fiscal/economic policy and wrote memos on proposed legislation to change the minimum wage and balance the budget

LEADERSHIP EXPERIENCE
Tufts Democrats, Vice President — September 2014 – Present
- Lead the largest on-campus student group; engage the student community in national, state, and local politics
- Plan issue-based panels, off-campus trips, and political organizing/voter registration efforts
- Launched a campus-wide campaign to promote legal protections for Massachusetts LGBTQ residents and led 100 Tufts students to canvass for Hillary Clinton's 2016 Presidential Campaign in New Hampshire

Inter-Greek Council Sexual Assault Prevention Task Force, Fraternity Representative — September 2016 – Present
- Educate students and implement compliance requirements for Greek organizations to encourage the prevention of sexual assault
- Work to change campus culture by increasing awareness of sexual violence prevention

Tufts University Admissions Office, Senior Interviewer — October 2017 – Present
- Interview and evaluate prospective high school applicants; provide student view of educational and extracurricular opportunities

Delta Tau Delta Fraternity, Philanthropy Chair — August 2016 – May 2017
- Led chapter to fundraise $14k for The Leukemia & Lymphoma Society; named Boston's collegiate fundraising champion

SKILLS/INTERESTS
- Proficiency in Mandarin Chinese
- Running, competitive tennis, foreign/independent films, and travel

Sample Interview Thank-You Note

Note: *A thank-you note should say something specific about the interview discussion and be sent via email no later than twenty-four hours following the interview.*

Subject Line of Email: Thank you for your time

Dear Hiring Manager,

Thank you for meeting with me this past Wednesday. I enjoyed learning more about the JPMorgan Compliance Department Summer Analyst program. Specifically, I am excited by the opportunity to work on special situations compliance issues and collaborate on projects on a Summer Analyst team. My academic record, communications skills, and my past internships in on-campus auditing and working on policy issues in government offices will serve my ability to contribute as a Compliance Summer Analyst at JPMorgan Chase & Co. I hope that you will consider my qualifications and experience favorably.

Sincerely,

Ken Smith
Ken.Smith@tufts.edu
(c) 928-555-5555

Appropriate Interview Attire for Men and Women

Interviews mean there is competition. A neat, appropriate self-presentation says, "This is important to me." Interviewers have personal preferences. When in doubt, do not wear it; take it out or cover it up. It is not worth the risk of potentially offending your interviewer. If accepted or offered a position, there is plenty of time to exemplify personal style.

COLLEGE INTERVIEWS

- Men: Unwrinkled slacks, button-down shirt, collared polo, blazer (optional)
- Women: Unwrinkled slacks, blouse, skirt, blazer (optional)

GRADUATE SCHOOL AND PROFESSIONAL JOB INTERVIEWS

- Men: Unwrinkled slacks, button-down shirt, collared polo, blazer (optional depending on type of interview). Suits, ties, dress shoes, socks, and belts are required for banking, legal, consulting, medical school, MBA, and PhD interviews.
- Women: Unwrinkled slacks, blouse, skirt, blazer

(optional). Pant suits or skirts and jackets with low or mid-heel pumps are highly recommended for banking, legal, consulting, medical school, MBA, and PhD interviews.

ATTIRE/STYLES TO AVOID FOR ALL INTERVIEWS

Short skirts, super-high heels, intense makeup, big earrings, excessive jewelry, unkempt hair, dirty sneakers, flip flops/sandals, and gum (especially for banking, law, consulting, and professional school) are to be avoided at all costs.

In college and creative fields (i.e. art school, chefs/cooks, entertainment, advertising, tech), dress codes are more relaxed; tattoos, piercings, and jeans are acceptable.

Coming Soon from the Communication Series for the Texting Generation

From Shake to $hake: Interview Storytelling Blogs for GenText™

About the Author

Elaine Rosenblum is the founder and chief articulation officer at ProForm U. At the intersection of advancing technology and diminishing human contact, Elaine combines her corporate and legal expertise to realize her vision that collaborative communication skills, both verbal and written, are the most valuable professional skills in the knowledge economy.

Foreseeing the impact of technology on communication,

in 2001 Elaine founded Courageous Conversation. She cofounded Access Test Prep & Tutoring in 2006. ProForm U serves the communication needs of both by teaching collaborative communication, articulation, and negotiation skills to students and seasoned professionals.

Elaine is a graduate of The University of Texas at Austin and Cardozo School of Law in NYC. During a yearlong law school mediation clinic, she mediated in the New York state courts and studied negotiation and collaboration theory. She also completed Harvard Law School's Advanced Negotiation program for lawyers. Elaine is an expert in creative problem solving, collaborative negotiation, and conflict management in the corporate environment. She is often quoted on Forbes.com for her expertise in improving communication in the corporate environment.